Ants for beginners

By Thorsten Hawk

Content

1. What are ants?

Ants are small insects that are part of the family Formicidae. There are more than 12,000 known species of ants that are found in almost every part of the world except Antarctica.

Ants are social insects and live in colonies or states that can consist of thousands of individuals. Each colony has a hierarchy in which one or a few queens run the brood nest while the workers gather food, build the nest, and care for the brood.

Ants have an elbow-shaped head, a short stalk, and a longer abdomen. They also have pincer-like mouthparts that they use to grasp and crush food. Most species of ants are vegetarians, although some species hunt insects or small animals.

Ants also have the ability to produce and use pheromones to promote communication within the colony. This helps them share the location of food sources and coordinate nest building and brood care.

In general, ants are an important part of the ecosystems in which they live and play an important role in regulating insect populations and maintaining soil structures.

2. Family, genera and species

Ants belong to the family Formicidae and are one of the most abundant insect species on Earth. There are thousands of different species of ants found in almost every part of the world.

Some well-known genera of ants are:

Atta: This genus includes the famous leafcutter ants that build large colonies and gather leaves for food.

Camponotus: This genus includes the wood ants that often live in tree trunks and branches.

Formica: This genus includes the red wood ants that are often found in European forests.

Solenopsis: This genus includes fire ants, which are often found in warm regions such as the southern part of the United States.

Each type of ant has a specific role within its colony. Some ants serve as gatherers, others as builders or warriors. The queen is responsible for laying eggs, ensuring the continuity of the colony.

Ants have a very social nature and work together to protect and feed their colony. Their organization and ability to cooperate makes them a remarkable example of social behavior in insects.

3. Natural habitat

Ants are very widespread in nature and are found in a variety of different habitats. A natural habitat for ants can be virtually anywhere there is adequate food and protection from the elements. This includes tropical rainforests as well as deserts, grasslands, and even in and around human settlements.

In tropical rainforests, ants are an important part of the ecosystem, helping to keep the forest free of pests and maintain its natural cycle. Here they can live in the tree trunks and branches, on the ground, or in nests underground. Some species also build their nests directly in tree canopies to take advantage of light conditions and moisture in the forest.

In deserts, ants can survive in extreme conditions because of their ability to collect and store water and food. Here they live in small nests under the ground, in plants, and in rock crevices.

Grasslands also provide a natural habitat for ants, especially for those species that feed on plant juices. Here they may live in small nests under the ground or in plants.

Ants can also often be found in and around human settlements, as they take advantage of proximity to food sources such as garbage, food scraps, and gardens. Here they often build their nests under sidewalks, in walls, or in buildings.

Overall, ants can survive in a variety of different habitats and are an important part of the ecosystems in which they live. They help keep nature in balance and maintain the natural cycle.

4. Anatomy of the ant

Ants are insects that have complex anatomy that allows them to survive and prosper in their natural habitats. An important part of their anatomy is their body, which is divided into three main sections: head, thorax, and abdomen.

The ant's head is large and compact and carries most of its sensory organs, including eyes, antennae, and mouthparts. The ant's eyes are spherical and allow it to perceive its surroundings. The antennae are long, movable structures that give it a better understanding of its surroundings and environment. The ant's mouthparts are essential for handling its food and building nests.

The ant's thorax is the middle section of its body and supports its six legs and two wings. The ant's legs are particularly adaptable and allow it to run fast and carry heavy loads. The ant's wings are used only for reproduction and are not intended for flight.

The ant's abdomen is the rear section of its body and houses its internal organs, including its digestive and reproductive systems. An important part of the abdomen is also their gaster, which serves as a storehouse for food and other important substances.

Another important part of the ant's anatomy is its exoskeleton, a hard outer shell that protects and supports its body. The hard exoskeleton layer is formed from chitin, a natural substance that makes their body strong and durable.

Overall, the ant's anatomy is a complex system that helps it survive and prosper in its natural habitat. Through their adaptability and ability to respond to their environment, they have managed to become a successful species.

5. Which ant species is right for me?

If you are thinking about keeping ants as pets, it is important to know that there are many different species of ants, each with their own needs and requirements. To choose the right species for you, you should familiarize yourself with the different options and decide which one best fits your lifestyle and resources.

Some of the most popular ant species kept as pets are:

Lasius niger (black wood ant): This species is a good choice for beginners because it is easy to care for and has a low potential to spread indoors.

Camponotus pennsylvanicus (Red Wood Ant): This species is known for its striking color and size, but it requires more care and attention than other species.

Solenopsis invicta (Red-winged ant): This species is not the best choice for beginners due to its high mobility and more aggressive nature. However, it is recommended to keep them in a special container to avoid spreading them in the home.

Formica fusca (Brown Wood Ant): This species is known for its ability to form large colonies, but it requires a larger terrarium and more care than other species.

Pheidole megacephala (Giant Head Ant): This species is known for its unusual size and coloration and can be easily kept.

Important factors to consider when choosing the right ant species are:

Your experience with caring for ants: If you have never kept ants before, you should start with a simple species such as the black wood ant.

Available resources: some species require a larger terrarium and more complex facilities, while others can get by with a simple terrarium.

Your personal preferences: Consider whether you prefer a larger or smaller ant species, a particular color or shape, or a species with special abilities such as the ability to fly.

Climate and environment: some species require certain climatic conditions to stay healthy and may become sick or die if conditions are unfavorable. Be sure to select a species that is suitable for your climate and environment.

It is also important to note that some species are considered endangered or protected and therefore cannot be kept as pets. Check the applicable laws in your state before selecting an ant species.

If you are unsure about which ant species is right for you, we recommend contacting an experienced breeder or organization such as a shelter or pet store. These experts can help you choose the right ant species and assist you with any care issues.

In summary, choosing the right ant species for you is an important decision that should be carefully considered. Review your resources, your preferences, and the climate in which you live, and seek assistance from an expert if needed to ensure that you select the right species for your needs.

6. Keeping black forest ant

Keeping Black Wood Ants requires some special considerations and precautions, as they are a very active species and need a specific environment to stay healthy and happy.

Enclosure: A suitable enclosure for Black Wood Ants should be at least 20 inches long, wide and high to provide them with enough room to move around. It is best to use a glass or acrylic terrarium that is well ventilated and allows enough light to pass through. A blanket of foam or Styrofoam can be attached to the top of the terrarium to create a comfortable climbing surface for the ants.

Furnishings: a combination of soil, sand and damp kitchen paper should be provided as a base within the terrarium. This will serve as a nesting area for the ants and keep the terrarium moist and beautiful. Plants or similar items can be added to create a natural and attractive environment.

Water and Moisture: Black forest ants need water regularly to stay healthy. A water source, such as a damp cotton ball or bowl of water, should always be provided. It is important to spray the terrarium regularly to maintain adequate humidity.

Feeding: black wood ants require a balanced diet consisting of various types of insects and small vegetables. Once a week, a small amount of honey or sugar water can be offered as an additional source of energy. It is important to make sure that feeding is regular and that any uneaten food is removed quickly to avoid contamination in the terrarium.

Temperature: black wood ants prefer a constant temperature of 23-27°C. It is important to provide a heating source to maintain the temperature in the terrarium.

7. Keeping red wood ant

The red wood ant (Camponotus pennsylvanicus) is a popular species among insect collectors and hobby beekeepers. They are characterized by their red coloration and their size of about 10-14 mm. In their natural habitat they build their nests in wood, but in captivity they can be kept in special ant farms or in artificial nests.

To ensure good husbandry for your red wood ant, you should consider a few important factors.

Temperature: Red wood ants should be offered a constant temperature between 21 and 29 degrees Celsius. It is important that the temperature does not fluctuate too much, as this can affect the colony's well-being and health.

Humidity: Adequate humidity is also of great importance for keeping red wood ants. Relative humidity should be around 60-70% to ensure a healthy climate in their nest. This can be achieved by regular spraying with water or by using a humidity regulator.

Nest: Red wood ants need a spacious and well ventilated nest in which to raise their brood and house their queen room.

There are special artificial nests for ants available commercially, or you can make your own nest from natural wood.

Diet: Red wood ants require a balanced diet consisting of sugar solutions, proteins (such as insects or meat), and vegetable matter. It is important that the diet is provided regularly to ensure healthy growth and a high survival rate of the colony.

Hygiene: cleaning and disinfecting the nest and equipment is also of great importance. This helps to reduce the risk of diseases and parasites and increase the well-being of the colony.

8. Giant head ant husbandry

Keeping giant headed ants (Camponotus gigas) is an interesting challenge for ant lovers. This species is known for its large head and relative size compared to other ant species. However, it is important to note that giant-headed ants have special needs and requirements that must be met to ensure that they can live healthy and happy lives in their environment.

One of the most important factors in keeping giant headed ants is the nest. A nest should provide enough space for the ants to move around freely, and should also provide enough moisture and warmth to create an ideal living environment. A good nest for giant head ants should be made of clay or clay bricks that meet the moisture and temperature needs of this species.

Another important factor in keeping giant-headed ants is diet. This species is generally carnivorous and requires a balanced diet consisting of insects, small vertebrates, and occasionally plant foods. It is important that the diet is varied and contains sufficient nutrients to support the health of the ants.

It is also important that the environment is safe and secure for giant headed ants. This species is susceptible to stress and can become ill if conditions are unpleasant. Therefore, it is important that the nest and environment are stable and secure to provide a safe and secure home.

Another important factor in keeping giant-headed ants is hygiene. It is important that the nest and surrounding area be cleaned regularly to provide a clean and healthy environment. It is also important that the water provided to the ants is changed regularly to ensure good water quality.

9. Formicarium and space requirements

A formicarium is the home for your ant colony. It is important that the formicarium has the right space requirements and conditions for your ants to stay healthy and happy.

A formicarium is a plastic or glass enclosure designed specifically for keeping ants. It is an ideal place for ants to live and build their nest. A formicarium can be made of different materials, but the most common material is acrylic or glass because it is durable, transparent and easy to clean.

A formicarium can consist of two main parts: the nest area and the arena. The nest area is where the ants will build and store their nest. Here you can either provide an artificial environment with moist substrate and materials for the ants to build their nest themselves, or you can provide an already built nest.

The arena is the area where the ants can perform their activities, such as gathering food or fighting other colonies. The arena may also contain a variety of landscaping and obstacles to encourage ant activity.

An arena should be large enough to provide the ants with enough space to climb, dig, and build camps. However, the floor should not be covered too high with soil to prevent migration from the nest to the arena. The size of the arena depends on the number of ants you are keeping, but as a guideline, it should be at least three times the size of the nest.

An arena should also contain a variety of landscape elements, such as rocks, trees, plants, and sandy areas. These elements provide shelter and opportunities for the ants to explore and hide in their surroundings.

It is important that the formicarium has good ventilation to ensure that the ants get adequate oxygen. It is also important that there is a way to regulate the humidity level in the formicarium, as too much moisture can damage the nest and the ants.

A formicarium can be equipped with a variety of accessories, such as a heater to keep the nest at a constant temperature, lighting to provide adequate light for the inhabitants, and humidity control to regulate the humidity level in the formicarium.

It is important to clean the formicarium regularly to ensure that the nest is clean and sanitary and that there is no fungus or mold growth.

A formicarium is a great way to keep ants at home and observe their activities. It is also a great learning tool for children and adults to learn more about ant biology and behavior. There are a variety of different types of formicariums available, so you can make a choice that fits your needs and desires.

When buying a formicarium, it is important to make sure it is the right size for the number of ants you want to keep. A formicarium that is too small can cause the ants to be overcrowded and not have enough room to build their nest and develop.

Size

The size of the formicarium depends on the size of your ant colony. A small colony will need a smaller formicarium than a large colony. As a general rule, a colony of 500 worker ants needs a formicarium at least 20 cm long, 15 cm wide and 15 cm high. However, if you have room for a growing colony, it is best to choose a larger formicarium to allow the colony to develop and expand.

Material

The formicarium should be made of materials that are durable and safe for your ants. Acrylic and glass are good options because they are easy to clean and maintain and provide a good view of your ants. Avoid using formicariums made of wood or cardboard, as these materials are porous and more susceptible to pests.

Furnishings

Within the formicarium, there should be ample space for your ants to build and run. Provide a layer of fine sand or fine gravel to cover the floor. Also add several logs or branches so that your ants have a structure to climb and build on. A water reservoir should also be provided so your ants have access to fresh water.

Ventilation

Adequate ventilation is important to ensure that your ants get fresh air. Make sure the formicarium has at least one opening for air circulation. If possible, you can also install a small fan to ensure constant air circulation.

Temperature and humidity

Ants prefer a warm and humid environment. Keep the formicarium at a constant temperature between 25 and 30 degrees Celsius and humidity between 50 and 60%. Use a thermometer and hygrometer to monitor the temperature and humidity in the formicarium and adjust if necessary.

Light

Ants do not require artificial light, as they have their own ability to detect and use light sources. However, it is important that the formicarium receives adequate natural light to ensure that the plants you provide for your ants can thrive. Place the formicarium in a bright, but not direct sunlight location.

In summary, it is important that you think carefully about the space requirements and conditions in the formicarium to ensure that your ants stay healthy and happy. A well-designed formicarium will provide many years of enjoyment for you and your ants.

10. Substrate and which soil?

An important requirement for successfully keeping ants at home is the proper substrate and type of soil. The soil should be kept moist so that the ants can find moisture and air in their nest. However, it is important that it does not get too wet as this can lead to rot. A good way to keep the soil moist is to use a layer of hydrocorrels or peat moss.

The type of soil used depends on the type of ant being kept. Some ant species prefer sandy soils, while others prefer moister soils. It is important to learn about the needs of your ant species and choose the right type of soil.

For most species of ants, a mixture of potting soil, sand and leaves is suitable. This mixture can be kept moist to meet the ants' needs while providing a good base for nest building.

It is also important to make sure that there are no pesticides or other chemicals in the soil, as this can be harmful to the ants. It is best to use biodegradable and untreated soil to minimize the risk to the ants' health.

In summary, the soil should be kept moist and the right type of soil should be used to meet the needs of each ant species. It is important to use biodegradable and untreated soil and to avoid the use of pesticides and other chemical substances to protect the health of the ants.

11. Planting

An important component in the design of the ant formicarium is planting. Not only can this help the terrarium look appealing to the ants, but it can also play an important role in maintaining a natural habitat for them. There are a variety of plants that are suitable for ants and can create a harmonious balance in their habitat.

One of the most important considerations when choosing plants is their moisture needs. Since ants prefer a moist environment, the plants you choose should also have high moisture absorption. Some good options are ferns, mosses and algae. These plants can help keep the terrarium moist while simulating a natural habitat for the ants.

Another important consideration when choosing plants is their resistance to pests. Some plants can be easily attacked by insects, which can lead to a messy environment and stress for the ants. It is therefore advisable to choose hardy plant species such as epiphytes, orchids and succulents that are less susceptible to pests.

It is also important to note that some plants can be poisonous, especially to ants. Therefore, you should always make sure that the plants you choose are not toxic and will not have any harmful effects on the health of your ants.

Finally, it is important that the planting is arranged to meet the needs of your ants.

This means that the plants should be arranged to create a natural habitat for the ants and provide them with space to move around freely. It is also advisable to create a few hiding places for the ants to retreat and feel safe.

If you have decided to keep ants at home, it is important that you also think about their environment. Plants can play an important role in creating a suitable habitat for your ants.

A good choice to start with are native plants that already communicate with ants in the wild. These plants not only provide a natural habitat for ants, but also food and shelter. An example of this is the oak tree, which is home to many species of ants.

Another important factor is humidity. Ants need a certain level of humidity to survive, and plants can help regulate that humidity in the terrarium. For example, watering plants or placing trays of water can maintain a constant humidity in the terrarium.

It is also important to choose plants that are appropriate for the size of your terrarium and the number of ants you have. Do not choose plants that are too large, as this can restrict the movement of your ants. It's also important that the plants don't cast too much shade, as this can affect the development of your ants.

Additionally, you should also make sure that the plants are suitable for use in the terrarium. Some plants are toxic or can have other negative effects on your ants. Therefore, it is important to research carefully before choosing plants.

Some of the most suitable plants for use in ant terrariums include:

Ficus pumila (climbing plant).

Ficus elastica (rubber tree)

Hedera helix (ivy)

Pteris cretica (fern)

12. Lighting conditions

Lighting conditions

An important component of caring for ants at home is lighting. Lighting plays a critical role in the well-being and survival of the ant colony. In this chapter, we will examine the various aspects of lighting conditions when keeping ants.

Type and duration of light

Ants are diurnal and therefore require sufficient brightness to carry out their activities. It is important to provide an adequate light source that is on for at least 12 hours a day. The best light sources are LED lamps or fluorescent fluorescent tubes, as they do not emit heat and therefore do not affect the humidity and temperature in the terrarium.

Intensity of light

The intensity of the light is also important. Too high a brightness can cause stress and discomfort for the ants, while too low a brightness can result in slowed activity and possibly even a reduction in reproductive rate. It is best to use a medium-brightness light source that provides even illumination throughout the terrarium.

Color of the light

The color of the light is also important. It is known that blue light stimulates ant activity, while red light calms them. Therefore, it may be helpful to use a combination of blue and red light to achieve the best results.

Light intensity

It is also important to note that the light falling on the ants should not be too strong. Too much light intensity can damage the ants' eyes and lead to a reduction in their ability to detect light. Therefore, it is important to maintain a sufficient distance between the light source and the terrarium to ensure adequate light intensity.

There is no exact distance that should be maintained between the light source and the terrarium, as this depends on several factors, such as the size and construction of the terrarium, the intensity and type of light source, and the specific needs of the ant colony. However, it is advisable to choose a distance that provides adequate light intensity without the light being too strong for the ants. As a rule, it is advisable to choose a distance of at least 30 cm. However, it is always advisable to observe the ants' reactions and, if necessary, change the distance to provide the best possible lighting conditions for the colony.

In summary, light conditions are an important factor in keeping ants at home. To create a healthy and active ecosystem for the ant colony, it is important to provide an adequate light source that is on at least 12 hours a day. The intensity, color and strength of the light should be carefully monitored to avoid stress and harm to the ants. By making the lighting conditions optimal, the well-being and survival of the ant colony can be improved.

13. Temperature

Temperature is an important factor in the health and well-being of the ant colony. Each ant species has its own preferred ambient temperature, but in general the ideal temperature for most species is between 25 and 30 degrees Celsius. It is important to note that the temperature inside the ant colony must be controlled, as it may differ from the outside temperature.

Too low a temperature can cause a slowdown in the growth and development of the colony. It can also lead to a reduction in the fertility of the queen and a reduction in the number of eggs she lays. However, too high a temperature can have even worse effects, including dehydration and stress to the ants. In extreme cases, death of the entire colony can occur.

To ensure that the temperature inside the ant colony remains constant, a heater or air conditioner should be provided if necessary. Another way to regulate the temperature is to place the ant colony in a location where the ambient temperature remains stable, such as in a heated room. However, it is important to note that abruptly changing the temperature should be avoided, as this can cause stress to the colony.

A thermometer can be used to monitor the temperature inside the ant colony. This is especially important if heating or air conditioning is used to ensure that the temperature remains constant. It is also important to check the temperature regularly, especially during the colder months, to ensure that it remains in the optimal range.

14. Water and moisture

One of the most important things to consider when caring for ants at home is providing adequate water and moisture resources.

Ants need water to maintain body moisture and to dilute food for their larvae. However, it is important to note that too much moisture can be a problem as it is susceptible to mold and fungal development.

An easy way to provide water is to place a container with a small layer of water in the ant cage. It is important that the water surface is not high enough for the ants to drown, and that the water is changed regularly to avoid transmission of pathogens.

A drip effect, where water slowly drips from a source into the cage, can also be used to provide moisture. This can be accomplished by soaking a piece of absorbent cotton or sponge in water and placing it over the cage.

It is important to monitor the moisture content of the substrate in the cage and, if necessary, moisten it with a damp cloth or spray bottle. However, it is important that the substrate is not wet enough to promote mold and fungal growth.

A humidifier can also be used to increase the moisture content around the cage. This is especially useful when kept in a dry climate.

In summary, when caring for ants at home, it is important to provide adequate water and moisture to ensure their health and survivability. However, it is also important to monitor the humidity in the cage to prevent mold and fungal growth.

15. Starting a colony of black wood ant

Black wood ants are an interesting type of insect to keep as pets. Here is a guide to keeping black wood ants at home:

Shopping: Before you start keeping black wood ants, you need to buy one or more colonies from a reliable dealer. Check that the ants look healthy and are active.

Setup: An important requirement for keeping black forest ants is a suitable terrarium. It should be large enough to provide enough space for the entire colony, and it should be humid and well ventilated. A terrarium for black wood ants should be at least 50x50x50 cm to provide enough space for the nest and the ants' movements. Use substrates such as peat moss or litter to meet the ants' moisture needs. In the terrarium, a moist and acidic soil consisting of a mixture of expanded clay, moist peat and sand is best. It is important to keep the humidity constant to ensure a good microclimate in the terrarium. It is also advisable to occasionally add some foliage and moist leaves to replicate the ants' natural habitat. It is also important to provide a moist area in the terrarium where the ants can hydrate.

Feeding: Black forest ants need fresh food regularly, such as insects, fruit or vegetables. Make sure the food is fresh and provided daily. Monitor feeding to make sure all ants have enough to eat.

Black wood ants require a high protein diet to meet their needs. They can be fed insects, small worms, spiders, small pieces of meat, or even dried fruits and nuts. It is important to provide fresh food and change it regularly to ensure a balanced diet. It is also advisable to provide a source of water, as ants need it as well.

Black forest ants prefer mainly sweet fruits such as apples, bananas, grapes, plums, pears and nectarines. However, avoid sour fruits such as citrus fruits as they are intolerable to the ants.

However, offer some vegetables such as carrots, celery stalks or kohlrabi as food. It is important that the vegetables are fresh and untreated. Avoid using GMO products or those with pesticides as this can affect their health.

To provide water for black wood ants in the terrarium, you can provide a fine saucer or bowl of water. Make sure the water is fresh and clean and is renewed regularly. It is also important that the water is deep enough for the ants to bathe in. It is also advisable to place a small bridge or slide in the water to ensure that the ants can easily get in and out.

Hygiene: It is important to keep the terrarium clean and hygienic to avoid diseases and parasites. Change the food and water regularly and remove excess moisture.

Temperature: The optimal temperature for black forest ants is between 25 and 30 degrees Celsius. Avoid large temperature fluctuations as this can cause stress to the ants.

Light: To ensure that the ants receive enough light, place the terrarium in a bright location. Avoid direct sunlight as this can affect the humidity in the terrarium. You can also use an LED lamp that emits UV light. This can help the animals be more aware of their surroundings and be helpful for their health. However, it is important to make sure that the light is not too bright and does not excessively disturb the ants. It is also advisable to turn on the light only for a certain period of time during the day to simulate an appropriate day-night rhythm.

Communication: monitor communication within the colony to ensure that all ants are working well together. Good communication is important for the health and welfare of the entire colony.

Contact with other colonies: Avoid contact with other ant colonies to prevent aggressive interactions.

16. Life span at home with queen

If you want to keep an ant colony at home, it is important to know that a queen determines the life span of the colony.

The queen is the most important member of the colony and is responsible for reproduction. Without a viable queen, the colony will die and cannot survive. The queen is the largest ant in the colony and is usually much longer than the worker ants. Her only job is to lay eggs that will hatch into new ants.

The lifespan of a queen depends on many factors, such as species, environmental conditions, and health. In the wild, a queen's lifespan can range from several months to several years. However, in a controlled environment at home, her lifespan can be shortened.

It is important that the environment of the ant colony is kept appropriate. The temperature should be constant and there should be enough moisture for the eggs and larvae to thrive. It is also important that the ants have enough food and water available.

If you notice that the queen is dying or becoming ill, you must act quickly to increase the colony's chances of survival. It is best to buy a new queen and introduce her to the colony. Some species of ants will be able to produce a new queen, but it may take months or even years before the new queen is ready to lay eggs.

17. Trapping ants without a queen and keeping them at home

Keeping ants at home can be a fascinating and educational experience. However, to establish a functioning colony, it is important to capture a queen and possibly worker ants. However, it is also possible to build a colony without a queen by capturing worker ants and keeping them at home.

If you want to capture worker ants, it is best to do so on a warm, sunny day. Look for ant trails or anthills and watch the ants work and carry objects. Use tweezers or a sheet of paper to carefully pick up some worker ants and place them in a small, air-permeable container such as a jam jar or small plastic box.

Once you have captured the worker ants, you will need to provide them with the food and water they need. Ants need sugar to gain energy, so you can add a drop of honey or syrup to the container. Also, make sure there is a moist component in the container to maintain humidity. This can be achieved by soaking a piece of paper or cotton with water and placing it in the container.

It is important to note that worker ants cannot lay eggs, so the colony will not grow or reproduce without a queen. However, you can watch the worker ants continue their daily life and social interactions. Monitor the tank regularly and make sure the food and water are adequate.

On average, however, worker ants can survive for a few weeks to a few months if they are properly cared for. Therefore, be prepared for the colony to eventually die out and focus on observing and learning about the behavior and interactions of the captured ants.

18. Roles in the colony

In an ant colony, there are a variety of roles that are filled by individual workers. Each ant has its own role and is important for the survival of the colony.

Here is an overview of some of the most important roles in an ant colony.

Queen: The queen is the mother of all ants in the colony. Her main role is to lay eggs and thus promote the growth of the colony.

Workers: Workers are the ones who do most of the work in the colony. They gather food, build nests, care for the eggs and young, and protect the colony from enemies.

Soldiers: Soldiers are the defenders of the colony. They are larger and stronger than the workers and are responsible for protecting the colony from enemies such as spiders, beetles, and other insects.

Wood ants: Wood ants specialize in collecting plant juices and nectar. They climb trees and shrubs to gather these resources.

Heath ants: Heger ants specialize in tending mushrooms that are grown in the colony. These mushrooms are an important food source for the ants.

Scout ants: Scout ants specialize in finding new food sources and nests. They run out of the colony looking for new resources, which are then collected by other workers.

Mothers: Mothers are workers who take care of the eggs and young. They care for and feed the young until they are old enough to work for themselves.

It is important to note that each ant plays an important role in the colony and that the survival of the colony depends on all ants working together. A successful colony needs a balance between all roles in order to function well and thrive.

19. Diet and feeding intervals

A balanced diet is essential to the health and well-being of ants. It is important to know what types of foods are best for different types of ants and how often they should be fed.

Most species of ants feed on non-animal foods such as sugar water, fruits, vegetables, nuts and seeds. Some species also require animal proteins, which can be provided by insects or small spiders.

A combination of honey and water in a 1:1 ratio is used to prepare the honey-water mixture. Unlike sugar water, it has additional vitamins and minerals. Insects are also an important part of the diet, as they provide the larvae with the protein they need. If you want a more natural setting, you can place a pot of a lice-infested plant in the terrarium to make the environment more realistic.

The frequency of feeding depends on the type of ant, the age of the colony and the time of year. As a general rule, ants should be fed every two to three days. However, it is important to monitor how much food the colony is eating and whether they need to be fed more frequently or less frequently.

It is also important to keep food fresh and clean at all times to avoid spreading diseases and pests.

Old food should be removed as soon as possible and replaced with fresh food.

In summary, it is important that the diet and feeding interval for ants be carefully monitored and adjusted to ensure their well-being and health. A balanced diet, based on the needs of each species, is an essential factor for success in keeping ants at home.

20. Typical behavior

Ants are gregarious insects that live and work in large colonies. Within these colonies, they have a clear hierarchy, with queens, workers, and drones. Each of these ants has a specific task that helps the colony function and survive.

Workers are the most common ants and are responsible for building and defending the colony, foraging for food, and caring for larvae. They work day after day, without rest, to meet the needs of the colony.

Queens have the most important goal of laying eggs and producing a new generation of ants. Once hatched, larvae are cared for and fed by workers until they become adults and in turn become workers or queens.

Drones have a limited life span and serve solely to mate queens to produce a new generation of ants. Once their task is complete, they die.

Another typical behavior of ants is to communicate with each other. They communicate using pheromones, chemical signals they emit to let other ants know where to find food or to signal a threat.

Ants are also known for their ability to carry and organize large loads. When they find food, they lay a chemical trail for other ants to follow. This allows them to bring large amounts of food back to the colony quickly and efficiently.

To protect their colony, ants can also be very aggressive defenders. When threatened, they will quickly work together to eliminate the threat.

In captivity, when ants are kept in a terrarium, they can sometimes be prone to stress if their environment does not meet the needs of their colony.

21. Cleaning and intervals

Cleaning intervals

The frequency with which you should clean your ant colony depends on several factors, such as the size of the colony, the type of ant, and the type of habitat.

In general, you should clean your ants' habitat at least once a month. However, if you observe that the state is expanding rapidly or accumulating waste, you should clean more frequently.

Cleaning procedure

Cleaning the ant formicarium

The formicarium should be cleaned thoroughly on a regular basis. When doing so, it is recommended to use a mild detergent to protect the nest and furnishings from germs and bacteria. Avoid cleaners that contain toxic substances, as they can be harmful to your ants.

Remove all dead ants and change the substrate if it is dirty. Also make sure that all food debris is removed.

Cleaning the food bowls

The food bowls should be cleaned daily to prevent contamination and mold growth. Use warm water and a mild detergent for this purpose. Dry the bowls thoroughly before placing them back in the formicarium.

Intervals

To ensure good health and hygiene of your ants, check regularly to make sure they are getting enough water and food and that the formicarium is clean and dry. A good indication is to check every 2-3 days.

If you notice that your ants are no longer active or are behaving abnormally, you should act as soon as possible. You may have a problem with the formicarium that needs to be fixed.

In summary, you should take care of your ants regularly to provide them with a healthy and hygienic environment. Use mild cleaners and make sure the formicarium is clean, dry and free of dead ants. Check the food bowls daily and make sure your ants are getting enough water and f

In addition to cleaning the habitat, you should also replace the food source regularly to prevent mold and spoilage. It is also important that you offer the food in small portions to avoid overfeeding and spoilage.

22. Acquisition costs and running costs

There are some costs that you should consider in advance. These costs can be divided into acquisition costs and ongoing costs.

Acquisition costs:

Terrariums: The terrarium should be large enough to provide adequate space for the ant colony to live and work. Terrarium sizes and materials vary in price and quality, but you can already purchase good starter terrariums for around 50 to 100 Euros.

Ant colony: There is a wide range of different types of pet ants available here, at different prices. The cost of a new colony can vary from 20 to 200 euros or more depending on the species and the size of the colony.

Food: Ants require regular food, such as insects or sugar water. This food cost should be included in your annual running costs.

Additional accessories: you may need additional accessories such as lighting, heating, or humidity control for your terrarium. These costs can range from a few dollars to hundreds of dollars, depending on your individual needs.

Ongoing Costs:

Food: As mentioned earlier, ants require regular food. This cost can vary depending on the amount and frequency of food, but you should expect an annual food budget of at least 50 to 100 euros.

Cleaning: Terrariums require regular cleaning to ensure a healthy environment for your ant colony. These cleaning costs can be minimized by using paper or disposable wipes, but you should still expect annual cleaning costs of 10 to 20 Euros.

23. Winter rest

If you keep ants at home, you need to prepare for a special kind of rest during the winter. In winter, it is important for many species of ants to go into a type of hibernation to conserve energy and survive the winter.

During hibernation, many ants will stop their activities and curl up to stay warm. It is important to provide your ant colony with an appropriate hibernation environment to ensure they survive the winter.

Way to create the hibernation environment for your ants is to place the terrarium in a cooler room that is at least 10-15°C from late October to early March. It is also important that the humidity in this room remains stable and does not get too low or too high. It is recommended to use a hygrometer to monitor the humidity.

Another option is to cover the terrarium to minimize light and noise. You can also add thick layers of dry leaves or foliage to improve the hibernation environment for your ants.

During hibernation, you must also be careful not to disturb your ants. It is important that you do not open the terrarium and that you do not touch the ants. Disturbances can cause stress and interfere with winter dormancy.

It is also important to note that no feeding should take place during hibernation. Ants store food for the winter during this time and do not require further feeding.

Once winter is over and temperatures rise again, your ants will awaken from their winter dormancy and become active again. Make sure you provide them with an appropriate environment by placing the terrarium in a warm location and ensuring there is adequate light and air.

In summary, it is important to know that hibernation is an important part of survival strategies for ants. Make sure you provide an appropriate hibernation environment for your ants by moving the terrarium to a cooler location, monitoring humidity, covering the terrarium, adding dry leaves or foliage, and avoiding disturbances.

Also, remember that no feeding should occur during hibernation. Once winter is over, make sure you provide an appropriate environment for your ants by placing the terrarium in a warm location and providing adequate light and air.

24. Ant queen and breeding

One of the most important components of a healthy ant colony is the queen. As the only female ant in the state that can reproduce, the queen has the responsibility of reproducing and maintaining the colony. A healthy and productive queen is therefore paramount to the success of your ant household.

The breeding of a queen begins with the establishment of a new state. When a group of workers is ready to start a new state, they will relocate a young queen to a new nest. Here the young queen will lay her first eggs, which will be cared for by the workers. After a few weeks, the first larvae hatch and are fed by the workers. Some of the larvae will grow into workers, while others will develop into new queens.

When a new queen is ready to lay her eggs, she is cared for and fed by the workers. The queen can lay up to a million eggs during her lifetime, but it is important to note that not all eggs will grow into live ants. Some eggs may be malformed or fail to hatch, and some larvae may die before becoming adults.

When a queen dies or her ability to lay eggs declines, a new queen may be hatched by the workers. This process may take a few weeks or even months, but it is important that a new queen be replaced as soon as possible to ensure the continuation of the colony.

In order to maintain a healthy queen and a productive colony, it is important that you carefully monitor your ant colony and quickly address any problem that may arise. This includes making sure your ants are getting enough food and water, and that the nest is kept in an environment that is suitable for their needs. It's also important to regularly check for parasitic enemies such as mites and fungi that can affect the well-being of your colony.

If you want to successfully breed your ant colony, it is also important to understand the type of ant you are keeping. Each species has its own special requirements and needs, and it is important to understand these needs in order to build a successful colony.

It is also helpful to contact other ant keepers and exchange ideas with them. This can help you solve problems and get tips on how to effectively care for your colony.

The way the eggs are cared for does not necessarily determine what hatches from them. Rather, the species that hatches from the eggs is determined by the genes contained in the eggs. However, it may be that the care conditions given to the eggs and hatching larvae can affect their survival and development. Therefore, it is important to meet the needs of the ant colony to promote successful breeding and development of the colony.

It is possible for another ant within a colony to become the queen. This often occurs in those species where there are multiple queens within a colony or where the old queen dies or is no longer able to perform her duties. In such cases, another worker ant may lay her eggs and take over the role of queen. However, it is also possible that there will be a fight between different ants for control of the colony. Therefore, it is important to regularly check for signs of problems within the colony and resolve them early to maintain a healthy and productive colony.

Catching a queen ant while she is swarming is a challenge, but it can be done. Here are some tips that can help you:

Observe the ants' behavior: Watch the ants closely and try to predict when the swarm flight will occur. Most of the time the swarm flight takes place during the day when the weather is warm.

Prepare the catching vessel: Prepare a capture vessel large enough to hold the queen. Fill it with moist soil and a few leaves to create a natural environment.

Catch the queen carefully: use tweezers or a small scoop to carefully pick up the queen and place it in the catch container. Try to disturb the other ants as little as possible.

Monitor the queen: Monitor the queen closely and make sure she has enough moisture and food. It is also important that the capture vessel is well ventilated.

Start a new colony: The capture jar with the queen should be placed in a quiet and dark place for several weeks. Many species should not be fed during this phase. Once the queen is stable, you can start a new colony by providing her with a nest and arena.

It is important to note that it can be difficult to successfully capture a queen ant and start a new colony. It requires patience and practice, but it can be a rewarding and interesting project.

25. Ant bite and formic acid

Although they are usually peaceful animals, under certain circumstances they may bite or use their formic acid to protect their colony or themselves.

Ant Bite

Ants bite when they feel threatened or need to defend their colony. The bite can be unpleasant, but it is usually not dangerous. However, some species of ants, such as the bulldog ant, can cause painful bites, especially on people with sensitive skin.

If you are bitten by an ant, it is important to wash the affected area with soap and water and then apply an antiseptic solution. It is also advisable to apply a cold pack to the affected area to relieve pain and swelling.

Formic acid

Formic acid is a chemical produced by some species of ants to deter or kill their enemies. The acid can be unpleasant to humans and pets and cause skin irritation. In rare cases, it can also cause more serious reactions such as breathing problems or allergic reactions.

If you or someone around you is affected by formic acid, it is important that you rinse the affected area with water as soon as possible and seek medical attention if you notice any signs of an allergic reaction.

In terms of keeping ants at home, it is important that you keep their colony in a closed container to ensure that they do not come into contact with humans or pets. If you notice that your ants are showing aggressive behaviors, it is advisable to remove them or seek professional help.

26. Common diseases and first aid

If you keep ants at home, it is important that you know how to monitor their health and provide first aid if they become ill. Here are some of the most common diseases that can occur in ants, as well as steps you can take to support their health.

Fungal infections: Fungal infections are one of the most common diseases in ants. They are usually caused by damp or poorly ventilated conditions. If you observe that your ants have a milky coating on their bodies, they could be affected by a fungal infection. To combat this, you will need to improve the moist conditions in their enclosure and separate the affected colony from others to avoid spreading it.

Parasites: Parasites such as mites and bugs can take up residence in your ant colony and affect their health. To control parasites, you need to separate the affected colony from others and use an appropriate anti-parasitic agent. It is also important that you clean their enclosure thoroughly to ensure that all parasites are removed.

Dehydration: ants can become dehydrated if they do not have enough water available or if their enclosure is too hot. To avoid dehydration, make sure your ants have access to fresh water at all times and that their enclosure is properly ventilated and humidified.

Stress: Ants can also suffer from stress if they are disturbed or threatened. To avoid stress, do not disturb their enclosure too often and make sure there are no threats in their environment.

If you notice your ants getting sick, it is important to act quickly to support their health. Here are some steps you can take to provide first aid:

Isolation: immediately separate the affected colony from others to prevent the spread of disease or parasites.

Cleaning: Clean the enclosure thoroughly to remove any possible pathogens or parasites.

Humidification and ventilation: make sure the enclosure is adequately humidified and ventilated for the ants to avoid dehydration and fungal infections.

Feeding: Monitor their feeding and make sure they have enough to eat and drink.

Involving an expert: If you are unsure about how to treat your sick ants, you should consult an expert who can give you further instructions and recommendations.

It is important to note that it is always best to take preventative measures to avoid disease and other health problems in your ants. Make sure their enclosure is properly ventilated, humidified, and clean, and that they have enough to eat and drink. By following these simple steps, you can improve your ants' health and enjoy them longer.

Notes:

Imprint

© 2023 Randy Bolz

Sterndamm 17

12487 Berlin

Edition (1)

Cover design, Illustration: Randy Bolz
Editing, Proofreading: Randy Bolz
Translation: Randy Bolz
Publisher: Randy Bolz
Printers: Amazon Europe in Luxembourg